T0077932

UNLEASH THE GREATNESS IN YOU THROUGH THE WORDS OF GOD

ADELEKE DOMINION

authorHOUSE®

AuthorHouse™
1663 Liberty Drive
Bloomington, IN 47403
www.authorhouse.com
Phone: 1 (800) 839-8640

Published by AuthorHouse 11/18/2020

ISBN: 978-1-7283-6367-7 (sc)
ISBN: 978-1-7283-6366-0 (e)

Print information available on the last page.

Most assuredly, I say to you, he who believes in Me, the works that I do he will do also; and greater works than these he will do, because I go to My Father. And whatever you ask in My name, that I will do, that the Father may be glorified in the Son.

—John 14:12-13, NKJV

1

WHAT IS GREATNESS?

Ask yourself whether the dream of heaven and greatness
should be waiting for us in our graves—or whether
it should be ours here and now and on this earth.

–Ayn Rand

Maya Angelou wrote a book called, "*I Know Why the Caged Bird Sings.*" If you lock a bird up in a cage, the bird will start singing. What are the songs? They are limitations, frustrations, and unfulfillment, and so on. For many years, I lived my life like a bird locked up in a cage, but a few years ago, I refused to continue to live like that, and I intentionally destroyed that cage of limitations, frustrations, and unfulfillment. Right now, I am living my life to the fullest.

Perhaps you have been living your life like a bird locked up in a cage. My question for you is for how long you will stay in this cage of limitations, frustrations, and unfulfillment? This is your time to intentionally destroy this cage and start living your life to the fullest. Your life is big, and bigger than you can ever imagine. You were born for more. You were made for more. This is your time to unleash the greatness that is in you.

Oxford American College Dictionary defined *greatness* as "the quality of being great, distinguished, or eminent." Oliver Wendell Holmes once said that, "greatness is not in where we stand, but in what direction we are moving. We must sail sometimes with the wind and sometimes against it but sail we must, and not drift, nor lie anchor." You will never unleash the greatness that is in you if you are moving in the wrong direction. You must keep moving in the right direction.

It is God's will for His children to move into the greatness that God intends for them from the foundation of the world. God does not want you to be an average person. He wants you to pursue greatness and to leave your own unique legacy on earth. You are still alive because there is a unique seed of greatness God has put in you that this generation needs. The earlier you recognize this, the better. Therefore, you owe it to yourself to know your calling because your greatness is in your calling. Your calling is your purpose, and it is also the catalyst that will push you into your greatness.

God has already planned your greatness from the foundation of the world, but you must be ready to do what it takes and work hard to unleash the greatness in you. Everything will work out for good for you because you love God, and you are called according to His purpose (Romans 8:28).

Jesus Christ told us in John 15:16, NKJV:

You did not choose Me, but I chose you and appointed you that you should go and bear fruit, and that your fruit should remain, that whatever you ask the Father in My name He may give you.

Jesus Christ has chosen you for greatness and to bear good fruit. The only way your fruit will abide is for you to abide in Him and His Words.

God Is the Source of Greatness

Great is the LORD, and greatly to be praised; and His greatness is unsearchable. One generation shall praise your works to another, and shall declare your mighty acts.
—Psalms 145:2–3, NKJV

Our God is a God of greatness and the source of greatness. Therefore, we, the children of God with His Divine DNA, have what it takes to unleash the greatness that is in us. If you are not unleashing the greatness in you, you are disappointing God because you have everything you need to do it. This is no time to complain or to fit in with chickens and turkeys but to surround yourself with eagles who are ready to fly. This is because you are the product of your relationships. Your relationships are powerful forces that will shape your destiny.

How precious also are your thoughts to me, O God! How great is the sum of them! If I should count them, they would be more in number than the sand; when I awake, I am still with you.
—Psalms 139:17–18, NKJV

God's thoughts are precious, and great toward His children. His thoughts cannot be numbered. There are no limitations or restrictions on His thoughts.

God's thoughts are not our thoughts, nor His ways our ways. As the heavens are higher than the earth, so His ways are higher than our ways, and His thoughts than our thoughts (Isaiah 55:8–9).

God's thoughts gave birth to God's Words, and He used His Words to create the whole world. For you to unleash the greatness in you, you have to start thinking like God. You have to change your thinking pattern to that of God. This is because most of the time, the devil will try to inject thoughts of limitations, failures, lust, depression, unforgiveness, and so on into your thoughts. You can only overcome all these negative thoughts by thinking like God. You may ask me, *how can I think like God?* You can think like God by reading and meditating on the Words of God. You have to let God's Words become your food every day. Joshua 1:8, NKJV explains this better:

> This book of the Law shall not depart from your mouth, but you shall meditate in it day and night, that you may observe to do according to all that is written in it. For then you will make your way prosperous, and then you will have good success.

What is your vision in life?

Then the LORD answered me and said: "Write the vision and make it plain on tables, that he may run who reads it. For the vision is yet for an appointed time; but at the end it will speak, and it will not lie. Though it tarries, wait for it; because it will surely come, it will not tarry."

—Habakkuk 2:2–3, NKJV

What is your vision in life? Where do you see yourself in the next five years? Where do you see yourself in the next ten years? You need to have a short term and a long-term vision. You need to write the vision down on a paper and make it plain and run with it. You must back your vision up with faith in God and your own actions. You must continue to pursue that vision until it becomes a reality. At God's time, it will surely come to pass.

> *And a vision appeared to Paul in the night. A man of Macedonia stood and pleaded with him, saying, "Come over to Macedonia and help us." Now after he had seen the vision, immediately we sought to go to Macedonia, concluding that the Lord had called us to preach the gospel to them.*
>
> *—Acts 16:9–10, NKJV*

When apostle Paul had a vision that some people in Macedonia needed help, he immediately went to Macedonia with his friend to preach the gospel to them. He backed up that vision with action. Please, when God gives you a vision, you should back up that vision with action. You should run with it until it comes to fruition.

You Need Courage to Move into Your Greatness

Have I not commanded you? Be strong and of good courage; do not be afraid, nor be dismayed, for the LORD your God is with you wherever you go.

—Joshua 1:9, NKJV

When Moses died, God commanded Joshua to take over the leadership position. God encouraged him to be courageous so that he could lead His people. Joshua was going through a transition, and the only way he would be successful was to have courage. You need courage to unleash the greatness that is in you. Some people will look down on you and tell you that you will not be able to achieve your dreams. They will tell you that it is only in your head. You will need God's courage during this time to continue your journey. This is the time to believe the words of Les Brown when he said that, "It is not over until you will." You will win because God is on your side.

You Must Be Able to Overcome Hardship

You therefore must endure hardship as a good soldier of Jesus Christ. No one engaged in warfare entangles himself with the affairs of this life, that he may please him who enlisted him as a soldier.

—2 Timothy 2:3–4, NKJV

There will be many hardships on your way to your greatness. You must be able to endure and overcome these hardships. You have to believe God for the strength to overcome these hardships. Apostle Paul told his spiritual son to endure hardship as a good soldier of Jesus Christ. This simply means that he was not a good soldier of Jesus Christ if he could not endure hardship. Are you a good soldier of Jesus Christ?

You must be willing to overcome every hardship in your life through the spirit of God. People with a victim mentality cannot overcome any hardship because they believe the world owes them something, but people with warrior mentality will overcome their hardships because they know how to fight to get to their promised land.

Daniel and His Friends Paid the Price for Greatness

But Daniel purposed in his heart that he would not defile himself with the portion of the king's delicacies, nor with the wine which he drank; therefore he requested of the chief of the eunuchs that he might not defile himself. Now God had brought Daniel into favor and goodwill of the chief of the eunuchs. And the chief of the eunuchs said to Daniel, "I fear my lord the king, who has appointed your food and drink. For why should he see your faces looking worse than the young men who are your age? Then you would endanger my head before the king." So Daniel said to the steward whom the chief of the eunuchs had set over Daniel, Hananiah, Mishael, and Azariah, "Please test your servants for ten days, and let them give us vegetables to eat and water to drink. Then let our appearance be examined before you, and the appearance of the young men that eat the portion of the king's delicacies; and as you see fit, so deal with your servants." So he consented with them in this matter, and tested them ten days. And at the end of ten days their features appeared better and fatter in flesh than all the young men who ate the portion of the king's delicacies. Thus the steward took away their portion of delicacies and the wine that they were to drink, and gave them vegetables. As for these four young men, God gave them knowledge and skill in all literature and wisdom; and Daniel had understanding in all visions and dreams. Now at the end of the days, when the king had said that they should be brought in, the chief of eunuchs brought them in before Nebuchadnezzar. Then the king interviewed them, and among them all, none was found like Daniel, Hananiah, Mishael, and Azariah; therefore, they served before the king. And in all matters of wisdom and understanding about which the king examined them, he found them ten times better than all the magicians and astrologers who were in all his realm.

—Daniel 1:8–20, NKJV

Daniel and his three friends were among the Hebrews that were in captivity in Babylon. They were among those that were selected by the king to go through the three years of training because they were brilliant. The king would examine them and either accept or reject them to serve in the palace. The king commanded that these young people must be fed with the portion of the king's food. The king wanted them to have a taste of the palace's life. Some of the young people were happy and filled their bellies with the king's food until they couldn't think creatively. They were partying and having fun. They saw it as an opportunity to enjoy themselves. Daniel and his three friends disciplined themselves and refused to defile themselves with the king's food.

They paid the price for greatness by sacrificing and disciplining themselves by not eating the king's food, but they ate vegetables and drank water instead of wine. They prepared for greatness by studying for their classes. When some of the young people were going to parties and getting drunk, Daniel and his friends were doing research and studying everything they could lay their hands on. They also spent time praying to God three times a day and studying the Words of God to know the mind of God.

After three years, when it was time for the king to examine them, the king found Daniel and his friends to be ten times better than all other young people and all the magicians and astrologers in all his realms (Daniel 1:20). Therefore, Daniel and his friends qualified to serve the king. They unleashed the greatness that was in them through discipline and preparation.

I know you will agree with me that greatness will not fall on you. If you want to unleash the greatness in you, you must be willing, ready, and able to pay the price for greatness.

When Daniel and his friends paid the price for greatness, they emerged as the best in the country. Therefore, they could work in the most powerful office in that country.

The Doors of Greatness Are Open for You

For a great and effective door has opened to me, and there are many adversaries.
—1 Corinthians 16:9, NKJV

A great door of greatness has open for you, but there are many adversaries, problems, and issues of life that want to stop you from unleashing the greatness that is in you. The devil knows that you are a child of God. He will never roll a red carpet for you to move into your greatness, but he will fight you with everything he has, but he will not win in Jesus' name. The devil will use your past against you. He will use your mistakes against you. He will lie to you that you will not achieve greatness because of the family you came from. He will tell you that you do not have what it takes to achieve greatness. He will tell you that it is all in your head and will not happen. You must put the devil in his place through the Words of God. He is a liar. There is nothing good in him or about him. He lied from the beginning. He is the father of lies.

Nehemiah Moved into His Greatness

Those who built on the wall, and those who carried burdens, loaded themselves so that with one hand they work at construction, and with other hand held a weapon. Every one of the builders had his sword girded at his side as he built. And the one who sounded the trumpet was beside me. Then I said to the nobles, the rulers, and the rest of the people, "The work is great and extensive, and we are separated far from one another on the wall. Wherever you hear the sound of the trumpet, rally to us there. Our God will fight for us." So we labored in the work, and half of the men held the spears from day break until the star appeared. At the same time I also said to the people, "Let each man and his servant stay at night in Jerusalem, that they may be our guard by night and a working party by day."

—Nehemiah 4:17–22, NKJV

Nehemiah was a cupbearer for king Artaxerxes. He got the news that the wall in Jerusalem was broken down, and its gates were burned with fire. Nehemiah became sad and started praying to God to give him favor with the king so that the king could allow him to go to Jerusalem to build the wall. God answered his prayers by giving him favor with the king. The king allowed him to go to Jerusalem, and gave him the resources he needed to build the wall.

Nehemiah left all the comfort in the palace and went to Jerusalem to build the wall. The mess in Jerusalem became his calling. At times, fixing other people's mess may be your calling, and you will not be fulfilled until you do it.

When Nehemiah got to Jerusalem, he did not tell anybody about his vision of building the wall but went and examined it. When God gives you a vision of greatness, you do not have to tell everybody until that vision becomes fruition. This is because if people do not know where you are going, they cannot stop you.

After a few days, Nehemiah gathered the Jews and told them that God had impressed upon his heart to rebuild the wall. The people gathered and started working on the wall.

Immediately, their enemies, Sanballat, Tobiah, and the Arabs, stood up against them, saying that they would never be successful in building the wall. Nehemiah did not listen to them but commanded the people to continue to build the wall. He focused on his calling. He told the people that they should use one hand to work on the wall, and they should use the other hand to hold their weapons so that if the enemies showed up, they could take the enemies out of their miseries.

Nehemiah did not play with his calling. Please, do not play with your calling. Nehemiah and the people fought to build the wall, and they also fought to protect the wall. You will fight to unleash the greatness in you, and you will also fight to stay at the level of greatness.

Humility and Service Will Always Precede Greatness

Therefore whoever humbles himself as this little child is the greatest in the kingdom of heaven.

—Matthew 18:4, NKJV

There is a correlation between humility and greatness. Humility is the prerequisite for greatness in the kingdom of God.

> *But Jesus called them to Himself and said, "You know that the rulers of the Gentiles lord it over them, and those who are great exercise authority over them. Yet it shall not be so among you; but whoever desires to become great among you, let him be your servant. And whoever desires to be first among you, let him be your slave just as the Son of Man did not come to be served, but to serve, and to give His life a ransom for many.*
>
> *—Matthew 20:25–28, NKJV*

Jesus emphasized that anybody who wants to be great must be willing to serve other people. Jesus used Himself as an example, saying that He did not come to this world to be served, but to serve humanity and to redeem them with His precious blood.

Professor Cornel West once said, "You can't lead the people if you don't love the people. You can't save the people if you don't serve the people." This statement is the synopsis of the life and ministry of Jesus Christ. Jesus Christ has to love people before He could lead them to God. He loved humanity so much that He redeemed them with His precious blood. He went through the agony of the cross to set mankind free from the curses of the law. The first Adam brought death into the world, but Jesus Christ (the second Adam) brought salvation and redemption into the world. Jesus served humanity. He served them by feeding them with food, preaching the gospel of the kingdom of God to them, healing them and casting demons out of them, resurrecting them from death, and dying for their sins. Your greatness will be measured by the quality of your service.

Follow the Right Process

> *Most assuredly, I say to you, he who does not enter the sheepfold by the door, but climbs up some other way, the same is a thief and a robber.*
>
> *—John 10:1, NKJV*

Please do not compromise your principles and integrity on your way to your greatness. Do not manipulate reality, and follow the right process. If you manipulate reality, you will put yourself in trouble in future.

> *Do you not know that those who run in a race all run, but one receives the prize? Run in such a way that you may obtain it* (1 Corinthians 9:24, NKJV).

Apostle Paul emphasized in this scripture that we must run the race that is set before us with the mentality of winning. We must have a plan and warrior's mentality of winning every time. Please pursue your calling aggressively until you fulfill it. Your calling is a catalyst that will catapult you into your greatness.

You Must Die to Live

I affirm, by the boasting in you which I have in Christ Jesus our Lord, I die daily.

—1 Corinthians 15:31, NKJV

Apostle Paul knew that he could not fulfill his calling without dying every day. That was the only way he could be effective in doing what he has been called to do. If you want to fulfill your purpose, you must die to yourself. You must be willing to deny yourself and carry your cross and follow Jesus Christ. Your testimony is in carrying your own divine cross. It is not in someone carrying it for you.

What shall we say then? Shall we continue in sin that grace may abound? Certainly not! How shall we who died to sin live any longer in it? Or do you not know that as many of us as were baptized into Christ Jesus were baptized into His death? Therefore we were buried with Him through baptism into death, that just as Christ was raised from the dead by the glory of the Father, even so we also should walk in newness of life.

—Romans 6: 1–4, NKJV

Death is not just what will happen to us at the end of our lives, but we can die or learn how to die while still alive. There is a correlation between life and death. We must be willing to die so that we can live. We must die to our flesh so that we can live in the spirit. We must die to sin to live a life of freedom. This is because anyone who commits sin is a slave to sin.

We will never be able to unleash the greatness in us without dying to ourselves. We must die to anything that wastes our time so that we can focus on our calling and greatness.

Dr. Martin Luther King Jr. said, "I am willing not simply to live and die for an ideal. I'm willing to learn how to die while I'm alive, so I can live life more intensely and abundantly." What we can learn from this statement is that it is possible to learn how to die while we are still alive to be productive and live our lives to the fullest. We will never live our life to the fullest until we learn how to die. Dying at times is denying ourselves to fulfill our purpose. We can never have any significant breakthrough until we learn how to die so that we can live.

> *Then Jesus said to His disciples, "If anyone desires to come after Me, let him deny himself, and take up his cross, and follow Me. For whoever desires to save his life will lose it, but whoever loses his life for My sake will find it.*
>
> *—Matthew 16:24–25, NKJV*

Jesus emphasized that anybody who wants to follow Him must deny himself and take his cross. Jesus personalizes the cross. This simply means that my cross will not be the same as yours, but we must take our crosses and follow Him to experience victories in our lives. The simple truth from these scriptures is that there is no permanent victory until we die to ourselves and carry our crosses.

2

JESUS WANTS YOU TO DO GREATER WORKS

Most assuredly, I say to you, he who believes in Me, the works that I do he will do also; and greater works than these he will do, because I go to My Father. And whatever you ask in My name, that will I do, that the Father may glorified Himself in the son. If you ask anything in My name, I will do it.

—John 14:12–14, NKJV

Jesus Christ emphasized that if you put your faith in Him, you will unleash the greatness that is in you. Jesus also said that if you ask anything in His name, He will do it so that His Father can take the glory. Please put your faith and trust in God, and He will take you to a greater height.

There are twelve things you must take into consideration before you can unleash the greatness that is in you:

1. Think big
2. You are chosen for greatness
3. Use Your Imagination
4. Prepare for Greatness
5. What Is Your Calling?
6. Go The Extra Mile
7. You Must Be Consistent and Persistent
8. Examine Your Life
9. You Must Be Creative
10. What Is the Quality of Your Service?
11. Wisdom
12. Worship

3

THINK BIG

For as he thinks in his heart, so is he. "Eat and drink!" he says to you, but his heart is not with you.

—Proverbs 23:7, NKJV

What we think we will become is exactly what we will become. If we think we will make it, and back up those thoughts with our faith in God and our actions, we will make it. Our thoughts are the catalyst that will shape our destinies.

We must think big before we can unleash the greatness that is in us. We cannot think inside a box. We cannot put limitations on our thoughts. William Arthur was right when he said that, "Nothing limits achievement like small thinking; Nothing expands possibilities like unleashed thinking."

Commit Your Works to God

Commit your works to the LORD, and
your thoughts will be established.
—Proverbs 16:3, NKJV

If we commit our works to God, He will take the responsibility of establishing our thoughts. This will give us peace and takes pressure away from us. We must live a life of surrendering to God before we can commit our works to Him. We must surrender to Him in every area of our lives. If we want God to establish us, we should do what king David told his son Solomon in 1 Chronicles 28:9, NKJV: "……

Know the God of your father, and serve Him with a loyal heart and with a willing mind; for the LORD searches all hearts and understands all the intents of the thoughts. If you seek Him, He will be found by you; but if you forsake Him, He will cast you off forever."

Put Away Childish Things

When I was a child, I spoke as a child, I understood as a child, I thought as a child; but when I became a man, I put away childish things.

—1 Corinthians 13:11, NKJV

It is good to think like a child when someone is a child, but it is dangerous if an adult is thinking and acting like a child. This is the situation of many people. We must be willing to avoid childish things so that we can focus and concentrate on our greatness. I have seen a forty-five-year-old man acting like a kid by spending almost twelve hours every day playing video games. He can never achieve greatness with that kind of childish behavior.

Your Gift Will Make Way for You

A man's gift makes room for him, and brings him before great men.

—Proverbs 18:16, NKJV

Using the gifts that God has given us will bring us before great men and women. We must know our gifts because if we don't know them, we cannot use them. When God created us, He already planned our greatness. This was the reason He gave us the gifts to fulfill our purpose. Our gifts must be developed to fulfill our purpose.

Pursue Honesty In Everything You Do

We are all one man's sons; we are honest men; your servants are not spies.
—Genesis 42:11, NKJV

There is a correlation between honesty and greatness. We must pursue honesty in everything we do so that we will not destroy everything we work hard for. Please avoid cutting corners and manipulations of any kind.

4

YOU ARE CHOSEN FOR GREATNESS

You did not choose Me, but I chose you and appointed you that you should go and bear fruit, and that your fruit should remain, that whatsoever you ask the Father in my name He may give you.

—John 15:16, NKJV

Many Christians find it difficult to believe that it has pleased God to choose them for His glory and pleasure. God chose you to bear good fruits. The only way your fruits can abide is for you to abide in God and His Words.

> *I am the vine, you are the branches. He who abides in Me, and I in him, bears much fruit; for without Me you can do nothing.*
>
> *–John 15:5, NKJV*

You cannot do anything unless God gives you the strength and the power to do it. You are chosen for greatness. You are chosen for freedom. You are chosen to carry God's glory. You are chosen to be blessed. You are chosen to walk in authority. You are chosen to overcome the world.

You Are Chosen to Be Blessed

Blessed be the God and father of our Lord Jesus Christ, who hath blessed us with all spiritual blessings in heavenly places in Christ: According as he hath chosen us in him before the foundation of the world, that we should be holy and without blame in love: Having predestinated us unto the adoption of children by Jesus Christ to himself, according to the good pleasure of his will.

—Ephesians 1:3-5 (KJV)

I believe without reservation that the time has come for Christians to look and act blessed. This is because we are the salt of the world. It is God's will to bless and prosper us in every area of our lives.

You Are Chosen to Overcome the World

For whosoever is born of God overcometh the world: and this is the victory that overcometh the world, even our faith. Who is he that overcometh the world, but he that believeth that Jesus Christ is the son of God?

—1 John 5:4 (KJV)

"For whosoever is born of God" are the children of God who are redeemed through the precious blood of Jesus Christ, and they will overcome the world. "This is the victory that overcometh the world" refers to the death, burial, and resurrection of our Lord Jesus Christ. Therefore, if you have accepted Jesus Christ into your life as your Lord and Savior, you have the license to overcome the world. "Even our faith" simply means that you must put your faith in the Son of God before you can overcome the world.

Faith is an eternal gift from God. Faith is the unwavering tool of divine deliverance. You can never take dominion until you have faith in God. This Christian life is a life of faith. The just will always live by faith (Romans 1:17). You cannot please God without faith (Hebrews 11:6). What money is in this world is what faith is in the kingdom of God.

You Are Chosen to Take Dominion

Then God said, "Let Us make man in Our image, according to Our likeness; let them have dominion over the fish of the sea, over the birds of the air, and over the cattle, over all the earth and over every creeping thing that creeps on the earth."

—Genesis 1:26, NKJV

You have made him to have dominion over the works of Your hands; You have put all things under his feet.

—Psalm 8:6, NKJV

Dominion simply means to dominate or to exercise control over something. It is God's will for His children to take dominion over everything He has created. Dominion was the original plan of God for humanity. It was lost due to the sins of both Adam and Eve, but Jesus Christ came and paid the price for dominion through His blood.

Please develop the mentality of taking dominion over everything in your life. If you are a child of God and you are not taking dominion over life, you are disappointing God because He already made a provision for your dominion through the death, burial, and resurrection of His Son. You must take dominion over depression, poverty, sickness, laziness, complacency, pride, gossiping, and so on in your life.

5

USE YOUR IMAGINATION

Imagination is everything. It is the preview
of life's coming attractions.

—Albert Einstein

Imagination is from the word "image." We will never rise above the image we create for ourselves. Most things in life have to do with our imagination. We can predict our future through our imagination. Imagination is the ability to create a mental picture of what we want in life. The organ of our imagination is our minds. It requires focus and concentration.

We can imagine great and better things for our lives, and families, and businesses. We can use our imagination to fulfill our purpose and unleash the greatness that is us. We have to be bold and intentional about using our imagination. Meditation is one of the tools for using our imagination. Every major invention in history starts with imagination. Great music, great poem, excellent architectural design, a great life, great businesses, and great books start from people's imagination. We can create our own destiny, legacy, and reality through our imagination.

God Almighty is the source of imagination. God has a powerful imagination. He created the universe with His imagination. God created imagination and gives it to men and women to create their own reality. There is a correlation between greatness and imagination. If we imagine greatness and back it up with our actions, we will achieve greatness.

Jamie Paolinetti once said that, "Limit lives only in our minds. But if we use our imagination, our possibilities become limitless." This is true. If we use our imagination, our possibilities have no limit.

6

PREPARE FOR GREATNESS

By failing to prepare, you prepare to fail.

—Benjamin Franklin

If you do not prepare yourself, you will fail. You must live a life of preparation to be victorious and successful every time. Preparation is a foundation for any Christian who wants to be established in God. Anybody who despises the day of little beginning will not make it. In our daily life, we must not despise the day of a small beginning.

Preparation is a divine principle. When Jesus Christ was born, the next day, He did not start performing miracles. He prepared for His ministry for thirty years because He knew that His ministry would shake the foundation of the world. It was His ministry that redeemed mankind, but before He could start His ministry, He prepared himself for thirty years.

If you have a big ministry, you need bigger preparation, but if you have a small ministry, you need smaller preparation. Therefore, your preparations are supposed to be in correlation to your destination.

Another example of someone who prepared himself was king David. Prophet Samuel went to David's house, and anointed him as a king over Israel. Immediately, he went back to the bush to take care of his father's sheep because his time had not come. God prepared him in the forest. God helped him to kill a lion and a bear that wanted to kill his father's sheep. Because God could trust David with the sheep, God could trust him with the throne. God will never give you a big ministry if you cannot handle a small ministry.

David's father (Jesse) sent him to the field to give food to his brothers who were soldiers, but when he got there, there was goliath who was threatening the Israelites. When David saw this goliath, the first thing that came to his mind was that he would kill this crazy giant threatening God's armies. That was what happened. David told king Saul that he should allow him to fight goliath. David killed him with a stone. He could kill goliath because God had prepared him in the bush for years.

David killed goliath. Therefore, he could move into his greatness, and eventually became the king of Israel. You will never move into your greatness until you kill the goliath on your way to your greatness.

King Saul failed miserably because of disobedience to God's instructions. He also failed because he preferred the presence of people more than the presence of God and had no preparation. King David was successful because he followed God's instructions. He was a worshipper, he loved to be in God's presence, and he had a good preparation. Please prepare to unleash the greatness that is in you. It will never happen by luck but by good preparation.

It was J.B. Matthews who said, "Unless a man has trained himself for his chance, the chance will only make him look ridiculous." We are provided with opportunities from God every time, but if your opportunity comes and you are not prepared to make it use of it, that opportunity will make you look ridiculous. The opportunity may not present itself again.

The Wisdom of Ants

The ants are a people not strong, yet they prepare their food in the summer.
—Proverbs 30:25, NKJV

We can learn from the wisdom of ants. Ants are not strong but very smart. They prepare their food during the summer so that they can have food to eat during the winter when they are not able to go out because of the snow.

John the Baptist Prepared the Way for Jesus Christ

In those days John the Baptist came preaching in the wilderness of Judea, and saying, "Repent, for the kingdom of heaven is at hand!" For this is he who was spoken of by the prophet Isaiah, saying: "The voice of one crying in the wilderness: 'Prepare the way of the LORD; Make His paths straight.'" Now John himself was clothed in camel's hair, with a leather belt around his waist; and his food was locusts and wild honey. Then Jerusalem, all Judea, and all the region around the Jordan went out to him and were baptized by him in the Jordan, confessing their sins.
—Matthew 3:1–6, NKJV

The principle of preparation is the principle of the kingdom of God. John the Baptist had to prepare the way for Jesus Christ so that His path could be straight, and people could know His ministry. If Jesus Christ needed preparation, you, too, need preparation to be fulfilled.

7

WHAT IS YOUR CALLING?

For the gifts and the calling of God are irrevocable.
—Romans 11:29, NKJV

What is your calling in life? I mean your calling and not your career. I mean your vocation and not your job. What is it that you were born to do? Your calling is your purpose. It is your reason for existence.

Doctor Myles Munroe once said, "The greatest tragedy in life is not death but a life without purpose." Please think about that. Death is not the greatest tragedy, but it is a tragedy to have life and not know what to do with life. Whatever you are doing that is not your purpose is beneath you. God created you uniquely because of your purpose. You were born with a purpose, for a purpose, and to fulfill a purpose. Life without purpose is useless. Your purpose is a catalyst that will push you into your greatness. It is not late to fulfill your purpose.

You Are Called with a Holy Calling

Therefore do not be ashamed of the testimony of our Lord, nor of me His prisoner, but share with me in the sufferings for the gospel according to the power of God, who has saved us and called us with a holy calling, not according to our works, but according to His own purpose and grace which was given to us in Christ Jesus before time began, but has now been revealed by the appearing

of our Savior Jesus Christ, who has abolished death and brought life and immortality to light through the gospel.
—2 Timothy 2:8–10, NKJV

For you see your calling, brethren that not many wise according to the flesh, not many mighty, not many noble, are called. But God has chosen the foolish things of the world to put to shame the wise, and God has chosen the weak things of the world to put to shame the things that are mighty; and the base things of the world and things which are despise God has chosen, and the things which are not, to bring to nothing the things that are, that no flesh should glory in His presence.
—1 Corinthians 1:26–29, NKJV

God's calling upon your life is holy. The calling of God for your life is for His purpose to be fulfilled in your life. God does not call the mighty or people who are already fit that need no help. God called men and women who are not fit and make them fit for His glory. God will not need you if you are perfect to do what He has called you to do because you will be thinking you are doing everything through your flesh, and no flesh can take glory in His presence. God wants people who will depend on Him every time and in everything. God will increase His anointing in your life when you move into your calling.

Remain in Your Calling

Brethren, let each one remain with God
in that in which he was called.
—1 Corinthians 7:24, NKJV

If you want to be fulfilled in life, please remain in your calling. Do not let anything take you away from your calling. God does not guarantee your protection if you move out of your calling.

Then he waited seven days, according to the time set by Samuel. But Samuel did not come to Gilgal; and the people were scattered from him. So Saul said, "Bring a burnt offering and peace offerings here to me." And he offered the burnt offering. Now it happened, as soon as he had finished presenting the burnt offering, that Samuel came; and Saul went out to meet him, that he might greet him. And Samuel said, "What have you done?" Saul said, "When I saw that people were scatter from me, and that you did not come within the days appointed, and the Philistines gathered together at Michmash, then I said, 'The Philistines will now come down on me at Gilgal, and I have not made supplication to the Lord.' Therefore I felt compelled, and offered a burnt offering." And Samuel said to Saul, "You have done foolishly. You have not kept the commandment of the LORD your God, which He commanded you. For now the LORD would have established your kingdom over Israel forever. But now your kingdom shall not continue. The LORD has sought for Himself a man after His own heart, and the LORD has commanded him to be commander over His people, because you have not kept what God commanded you."

—1 Samuel 13:8–14, NKJV

God rejected king Saul because he walked away from his calling by offering a burnt offering that prophet Samuel supposed to offer. He was a king and not a priest. He disobeyed God because of the people. The kingdom was taken away from him.

I, therefore, the prisoner of the Lord, beseech you to walk worthy of the calling with which you were called, with all lowliness and gentleness, with longsuffering, bearing with one another in love, endeavoring to keep the unity of the spirit in the bond of peace.

—Ephesians 4:1-3, NKJV

Apostle Paul emphasized to us that we must live our lives worthy of our calling. This means we must pursue honesty and integrity in our lives. If you have been called to be a man or woman of God, please preach the Words of God with integrity and dignity. We must pursue excellence in every area of our lives.

What The Woman Gave Birth To Was What Redeemed Her

I will use an illustration that God gave me from what happened in the Garden of Eden. The devil walked into the coolness of the Garden of Eden and deceived Eve to eat the fruit God forbade them not to eat. She also gave the fruit to Adam, who ate it too (Genesis 3:1-6).

God cursed Adam, Eve, and the devil. If we take a critical look at what happened in the Garden of Eden, it was as if the devil won because both Adam and Eve lost dominion, which was God's original plan for humanity. They also lost the unique relationship they had with God.

The devil was happy and gathered a delegation of over two billion demons. They started dancing and jubilating because they thought they kept humanity where they wanted humanity, which was a place of bondage.

But before they could finish dancing, someone appeared on the scene. Who was this person? It was the Ancient of Days, Terrible Majestic, the Lily of the Valley, the Rose of Sharon, I am that I am, Almighty God. When the devil saw God, he was shivering because he could not handle God's glory. God told the devil that He could not react to what he did because He knew that human beings would commit sins and come short of God's glory, but a Precious Lamb had been slain for their sins from the foundation of the world. When the devil heard that, he was electrocuted with shock and electrified with agony. He was confused.

This was because he did not know that God had a plan. God also told the devil that he should look at the woman because the devil thought he had destroyed her life. She would go to hellfire, but God told the devil that the woman's seed would bruise the head of the devil.

The devil was sad because his plan failed. The plans of the devil will fail in your life and families in Jesus' name. The seed of the woman was Jesus Christ, who died for the sins of the world and resurrected the third day and finally bruised the head of the devil.

The woman was still weeping because she thought she was not going to make it. Immediately, God looked at the woman and told her, "Woman, stop crying; woman, stop weeping; woman, stop complaining because hope is on the way, and freedom is also on the way."

Then, God asked the woman a question: "What do you have?" The woman answered, "I have my seed." Then, God commanded her, "Give birth to your seed." The woman gave birth to her seed. It was that seed that God used to redeem, to deliver, and set her free from death. The seed was Jesus Christ, who redeemed the whole world with His precious blood.

God delivered the woman through what she gave birth to. God will deliver you through what you will give birth to or through your seed. What is the specific seed you were born to sow? If you think I am talking about your offering, tithe, and donation, you do not understand what I am talking about. I am talking about your calling. What is your calling? This is because your deliverance is in your calling, your blessings are in your calling, your breakthroughs are in your calling, your freedom is in your calling, your favor is in your calling, your fulfillment is in your calling, and your greatness is in your calling. You are running out of time. Your time has come to move into your calling. It is right now. It is not too late to give meaning to your life. God is waiting for your manifestation.

Charlotte Brontë Moved into Her Greatness

A good example of someone who aggressively pursued her calling was a lady called Charlotte Brontë, who was born on April 21, 1816, in Thornton, Yorkshire, in the north of England, and died on March 31, 1855. She lived a short life but left her unique legacy on earth.

Charlotte Brontë was the third child of Reverend Patrick Brontë and Maria Branwell Brontë. They had six children. Charlotte's mother died when she was young. Her auntie moved in to help raise her and her siblings. It was a sad time for this family.

Charlotte's elder sisters were Maria and Elizabeth. They died of tuberculosis due to the condition of their school. Charlotte Brontë took the leadership position of taking care of her siblings.

Charlotte and her siblings were unique in many ways. They were not used to entertainment like many kids, but they read and wrote a lot. They also lived the life of the mind and imagination.

Charlotte knew that God has given her a gift of writing. Therefore, she developed the gift no matter what was happening in her family. They were poor, but she did not let that stop her from preparing herself and developing her gift.

She traveled to Brussels to learn French and German so that she could start her own school to help kids and to also become an accomplished writer. It was difficult for her, but she refused to take her education for granted.

Charlotte published a book with her sisters Emily and Anne. There were only two people that bought that book. Charlotte was not discouraged but was happy that she had established herself as an author. She did not despise the day of little beginning. You, too, should not despise the day of little beginning.

Charlotte wrote another book called *"The Professor."* The book was rejected by many publishers because they believed it was not marketable. Charlotte did not give up. If you give up on your calling, you will not make it. Charlotte wrote another book called *"Jane Eyre."* The book was published and became a global success.

"Jane Eyre" was written over 161 years ago and is still a classic. This book simply transcends time. It is one of the best fifty fictions of all time. It is being read both in academic and non-academic environments. It is a mandatory book in secondary schools and many universities around the world. There were more than ten movies on *Jane Eyre*. All these were possible because Charlotte Brontë did not give up on her calling. She used her adversity as a ladder to her greatness. What she

gave birth to, catapulted her from obscurity into popularity. This is your time. The time you are waiting and praying for is right now. Please do not waste your time by pursuing shadow but must aggressively pursue God's calling for your life.

Thomas Paine Fulfilled His Purpose

Thomas Paine was born in England. He got married and messed up his marriage. He started his business, but the business failed. He got a job and got fired after a few months. He failed in almost everything he did. He came to America by the invitation of Benjamin Franklin. He started working as a publisher, and in less than a year, he wrote a book that changed America's fabric. The book was called *Common Sense.* It was this book that challenged the colonies to fight Great Britain for independence. His purpose was to write this book. George Washington commanded his soldiers to read *Common Sense* before fighting Great Britain so that they could be motivated. America fought Great Britain and won. This would not have happened if not for *Common Sense.* President John Adams once said that, "The sword of George Washington would have been raised in vain if not for the pen of the author of *Common Sense.*" He fulfilled his purpose by writing this book. *Common Sense* had catapulted him to his greatness. Some people called Thomas Paine, "The Father of the American Revolution." He deserved that. Thomas Paine achieved greatness through his purpose. You, too, will achieve greatness through your purpose.

8

GO THE EXTRA MILE

There are no traffic jams on the extra mile.

-- Zig Ziglar

You must be willing to go the extra mile before you can unleash the greatness that is in you. God has created you to be an extraordinary person. The principle of going the extra mile is the principle of the kingdom of God. When Jesus Christ was in the Garden of Gethsemane and saw what He had to go through to redeem mankind, He wanted to give up. He told God, "Let this cup pass over me" (Matthew 26:39, NKJV) because of His flesh. Everything would have been over with that statement because human beings would not have been redeemed by His blood. But Jesus Christ went the extra mile and said, "But let your will be done" (Matthew 26:39, NKJV). We know that it is the will of God for Jesus Christ to redeem mankind with His blood. Jesus Christ went the extra mile to redeem both you and me. To our God be the glory. You cannot have a serious breakthrough until you go the extra mile.

Zacchaeus Went the Extra Mile

Then Jesus entered and passed through Jericho. Now behold, there was a man named Zacchaeus who was a chief tax collector, and he was rich. And he sought to see who Jesus was, but could not because of the crowd, for he was of short stature. So he ran ahead and climbed up into a sycamore tree to see him, for He was going to pass that way. And when Jesus came to the place, He looked up and saw him, and said to him, "Zacchaeus, make haste and come down, for today I must stay at your house." So he made haste and came down, and received Him joyfully. But when they saw it, they all complained, saying, "He has gone to be a guest with a man who is a sinner." Then Zacchaeus stood and said to the Lord, "Look, Lord, I give half of my goods to the poor; and if I have taken anything from anyone by false accusation, I restore fourfold." And Jesus said to him, "Today salvation has come to this house, because he also is a son of Abraham; for the Son of Man has come to seek and to save that which was lost.

—Luke 19:1–10, NKJV

Zacchaeus was no ordinary man. He was a rich man who recognized the fact that he needed what Jesus had. He knew that Jesus would be passing by in a place. He knew he would not be able to see him because of the crowd and his small stature. Therefore, he did the unthinkable. He climbed a tree so that he could see the Messiah. It was unpopular for a rich man to climb a tree like a kid to see the Messiah.

When Jesus Christ got to the spot where he was, Jesus looked up and said, "Zacchaeus, make haste and come down, for today I must stay at your house" (Luke 19:5). Many people could not believe this because Zacchaeus was a sinner who took bribes from people.

The question we have to ask ourselves is *Why would Jesus do that?* The answer is that Jesus knew what Zacchaeus did.

He knew that he went the extra mile to see Him. Nobody has ever received salvation that way before. Salvation came to him and his families because he went the extra mile to see the Messiah. He received uncommon blessings for going the extra mile. If you want to receive uncommon blessings, please go the extra mile.

Apostle Paul Was A Great Man

Apostle Paul was also known as Paul of Tarsus. He was from the tribe of Benjamin and called himself a Hebrew of Hebrews. He persecuted the church before his encounter with Jesus Christ on his way to Damascus to persecute more Christians. This was what prompted him to say that he received the gospel from Jesus Christ and not from any human being.

He was a great man because he went the extra mile in everything he did for God's kingdom. He was not an ordinary apostle. He wrote two-thirds of the New Testament. He was not one of the original apostles, but he did more work than all of them. He was the apostle who God chose to preach the gospel to the Gentiles. He was the one who God used to plant many churches all over Europe. He was the one who took Christianity out of the box. He was the one who brought order and discipline into the churches through his letters and his messages. He taught Christians practical life in accordance with the will of God and faith in God.

He achieved many things in the kingdom of God because he went the extra mile. He pursued his calling until he fulfilled it. He was a prolific writer. He was an avid reader. He was an intellectual of intellectuals. He was a thinker of thinkers. He had powerful revelations about the kingdom of God. He had many spiritual sons whom he taught spiritual things. He knew that there is no success without a successor. Timothy was one of them. He challenged Timothy to study to be the best and to live a holy life in 2 Timothy 2:15–16, KJV:

> Study to shew thyself approved unto God, a workman that needeth not to be ashamed, rightly dividing the word of truth. But shun profane and vain babbling, for they will increase to more ungodliness.

If you want to unleash the greatness that is in you, please go the extra mile.

9

YOU MUST BE CONSISTENT AND PERSISTENT

Nothing in this world can take the place of persistence. Talent will not; nothing is more common than unsuccessful people with talent. Genius will not; unrewarded genius is almost a proverb. Education will not; the world is full of educated derelicts. Persistence and determination alone are omnipotent. The slogan "press on" has solved and always will solve the problems of the human race.

—Calvin Coolidge

There must be consistency in direction.

—W. Edwards Deming

You must be persistent and consistent in the direction you have chosen for your life. If you want to be productive and increase your momentum in your undertaking, you must be persistent and consistent. Consistency will always conquer all oppositions. What is distracting many people from moving into their greatness is the lack of focus and inconsistency. You cannot be efficient if you don't have a focus. You must believe in your own greatness and own it.

Persistence Will Always Yield Results

Then she said to him, "How can you say, 'I love you,' when your heart is not with me? You have mocked me these three times, and have not told me where your great strength lies." And it came to pass, when she pestered him daily with her words and pressed him, so that his soul was vexed to death, that he told her all his heart, and said to her, "No razor has ever come upon my head, for I have been a Nazirite to God from my mother's womb. If I am shaven, then my strength will leave me, and I shall become weak, and be like any other man."

—Judges 16:15–17, NKJV

This is a sad story. This is about Samson's fall, and he ended up perishing with the Philistines when he disobeyed God. But there is a lesson we can learn from this story. Samson connected himself with a lady who disconnected him from God. Samson fell in love with a lady in Gaza who was a prostitute, whose name was Delilah. Delilah had been offered a lot of money by the Philistines to entice Samson to know the source of his strength so that they could get him and afflict him and overpower him (Judges 16:5).

Delilah was persistent in asking Samson the source of his strength. Samson lied to her three times, but she continued to ask him every day until Samson was sick of it and told her the source of his strength. They finally got him. This was a breakthrough for Delilah because she got money from the Philistines. She could achieve this because she was persistent. You will have your own breakthrough if you are persistent.

Another example of someone who was persistent is a widow in the book of Luke 18:2–5, NKJV:

There was in a certain city a judge who did not fear God nor regard man. Now there was a widow in that city; and she came to him, saying, "Get justice for me from my adversary." And he would not for a while; but afterward he said within himself, "Though I do not fear God nor regard man, yet because this widow troubles me I will avenge her, lest by her continual coming she weary me."

This widow got what she wanted from this wicked judge because she was persistent. If you are persistent, you will get anything you want in life.

10

EXAMINE YOUR LIFE

Examine yourselves as to whether you are in the faith. Test yourselves. Do you not know yourselves, that Jesus Christ is in you? – unless indeed you are disqualified.
—2 Corinthians 13:5, NKJV

God wants us to examine our lives every day. This is because human beings can think and make decisions. They are not like animals that cannot think and make decisions. An unexamined life cannot be celebrated. If you want people to celebrate your life, you have to start living a life of critical examination so that you can get rid of all the unnecessary things and focus on your calling.

It was Socrates who said, "An unexamined life is not worth living." What Socrates did not add to his quotation was that it is difficult to examine our lives. When you start examining your life, and see all the mistakes you have made, you must make some changes and correct them so that you can move forward.

11

YOU MUST BE CREATIVE

In the beginning, God created heaven and the earth.

—Genesis 1:1, NKJV

We can never unleash the greatness in us until we learn how to be creative. Almighty God is the Creator. Therefore, we, the children of God have the innate ability to be creative.

We cannot increase our creativity if we are operating inside a box. We must get out of the box and start operating freely without restrictions. We can be creative by putting our faith in God so that whatever we will create will glorify Him. We can be creative by broadening our minds. This is no time to think old thoughts, but it is time to think big. We can be creative by exposing ourselves to new things we have not seen or done before.

12

WHAT IS THE QUALITY OF YOUR SERVICE?

Not everybody can be famous but everybody can be great, because greatness is determined by service.

—Martin Luther King Jr.

What is the quality of your service to God and humanity? Are you comfortable adding values to others by serving them? What is the quality of your service to your family? What is the quality of your service to your church? What is the quality of your service in your place of work? What is the quality of your service as a father? What is the quality of your service as a husband? What is the quality of your service as a mother? What is the quality of your service as a wife? What is the quality of your service as a brother? What is the quality of your service as a sister? I am asking all these funny questions because you can measure your greatness by the quality of your service to others and to God, at whatever level you are in your life.

An excellent example from the Bible is the chief priest called Aaron. Nobody can take it upon himself to become a priest. Only God can choose priests for the services of offering sacrifices for the sins of the people and their own sins, too, because they have weaknesses. God chose Aaron from the tribe of Levi to be the chief priest. God blessed Aaron and his families through the offering the Israelites gave to God.

God told Aaron specifically that he had no inheritance with the Israelites and God Himself was Aaron's inheritance

(Numbers 18:20). This was difficult for Aaron because he waited for this inheritance all his life. Aaron was faithful, serving God and the people of Israel for many years before he died.

After hundreds of years, God remembered Aaron's service to him. He chose Aaron's great, great, great-grandson to beautify His temple in Jerusalem. God also gave him favor with the king. The name of this man was Ezra.

The hand of God was evidenced in Ezra's life because he was chosen by God because of the seed of service that Aaron (his great, great, great grandfather) had sown. God protected him throughout his journey from Persia to Jerusalem (Ezra 7:12–18).

Another good example is Jesus Christ. The greatness of Jesus Christ can be seen in His service to God and to humanity. He came to the world not to seek His own will but to fulfill the will of His Father by taking it upon Himself to die for the sins of the world. He also served humanity by feeding them, healing them, delivering them, casting demons out of them, setting them free from bondage, and also preaching the gospel of the Kingdom of God to them. He was touched with the feelings of their infirmities (Hebrews 4:15). He reconciled them to God so that they can have a good relationship with God. Apostle Paul put it this way in 2 Corinthians 5:19, NKJV: "…God was in Christ reconciling the world to Himself, not imputing their trespasses to them, and has committed to us the word of reconciliation."

It was because of what Jesus Christ did that God has given him a unique name. At the mention of the name of Jesus Christ, every knee shall bow, and every mouth will confess that Jesus Christ is Lord (Philippians 2:10). His name is more beautiful than all the songs they are singing in heaven.

13

WISDOM

Science is organized knowledge. Wisdom is organized life.

—Immanuel Kant

Wisdom is the act of mastering life in accordance to God's will and expectations. Wisdom also refers to accumulated knowledge through experience. You can never embark on the journey of greatness without the wisdom of God. It is the wisdom of God that will establish your destiny. Please get wisdom and understanding.

In their book, *From Chaos to Coherence: The Power to Change Performance.* Doc Childre and *Bruce Cryer emphasized that,* "It is no longer enough to be smart—all the technological tools in the world add meaning and value only if they enhance our core values, the deepest part of our heart. Acquiring knowledge is no guarantee of practical, useful application. Wisdom implies a mature integration of appropriate knowledge, a seasoned ability to filter the inessential from essential." This is true. You need wisdom to get rid of unnecessary things and focus on what is important. This will help you to maximize your time and increase your productivity. Wisdom will help you to arrange your activities according to their importance. This means you will do the important work first before those that are least important. You must know that busyness or activities do not mean productivity. Please focus on being productive.

You Have to Fear God

And to man He said, "Behold, the fear of the Lord, that is wisdom, and to depart from evil is understanding."
—Job 28:28, NKJV

When you fear God, you are just beginning to act in wisdom. Your fear is based on submission to God and His will for your life.

> *The fool has said in his heart, "There is no God." They are corrupt, they have done abominable works, there is none who does good.*
> *—Psalms 14:1, NKJV*

The Word of God declares that anybody who does not believe in God has been condemned to the world of foolishness. God is the Creator of the universe, and He should be respected and worshipped.

Wisdom Is Calling You

Wisdom calls aloud outside; she raises her voice in the open squares. She cries out in the chief concourses, at the openings of the gates in the city she speaks her words: "How long, you simple ones, will you love simplicity? For scorners delight in their scorning, and fools hate knowledge. Turn at my rebuke; surely I will pour out my spirit on you. I will make my words known to you.

—Proverbs 1:20–23, NKJV

It is God's will for you to have wisdom. Wisdom is calling you, and you have to go get it. Wisdom will never fall on you. You must seek for it in every area of your life. There is always a price to pay for being foolish. God will not give wisdom to a fool because a fool cannot handle the wisdom of God. God will always give His wisdom to those who are seeking and are hungry for it.

Get Wisdom

Get wisdom! Get understanding! Do not forget, nor turn away from the words of my mouth. Do not forsake her, and she will preserve you; Love her, and she will keep you. Wisdom is the principal thing; therefore get wisdom. And in all your getting, get understanding. Exalt her, and she will promote you; she will bring you honor, when you embrace her.

—Proverbs 4:5–8, NKJV

Please get wisdom for everything you do in your life. Wisdom will give you honor and bring you before great men and women. To experience a breakthrough in every area of your life, you need wisdom. Wisdom will preserve you and keep you. The wisdom of God cannot be separated from the will of God. If you are seeking the will of God for your life, you are acting in wisdom. Wisdom will enable you to unleash the greatness that is in you.

The wise shall inherit glory, but shame shall be the legacy of fools.
—Proverbs 3:35, NKJV

The wise will have access to the glory of God, but foolish people's habitation will be desolation and shame. Wise people will always follow the directions of God, but foolish people will not. Foolish people like to deceive themselves.

Trust the Lord

Trust in the LORD with all your heart, and lean not on your own understanding; in all your ways acknowledge Him, and He shall direct your paths.
—Proverbs 3:5–6, NKJV

There is wisdom in trusting God. When you trust God, God will take the responsibility of directing your path. You will never fail when you put your absolute trust in God.

Guide Your Heart

Keep your heart with all diligence, for out of it spring the issues of life. Put away from you a deceitful mouth, and put perverse lips far from you. Let your eyes look straight

ahead, and your eyelids look straight before you. Ponder the path of your feet, and let all your ways be established.
—Proverbs 4:23–26, NKJV

Guide and keep your heart from pollution and bad thoughts because out of it will flow the issues of life. Thoughts of invention and greatness will flow from your heart. Plan ahead for your future, and God will direct your path. You must be actively involved in what is going on in your life. You must be aware of what is going on around you. Foolish people are unaware and clueless. They are always surprised because they do not plan their lives.

He who guards his mouth preserves his life, but he who opens wide his lips shall have destruction.
—Proverbs 13:3, NKJV

It is a breakthrough if you can guide your mouth. Before you talk, you must be able to think so that you will not say anything that does not make sense. People that cannot guide their mouths always find themselves in trouble because they will say things they are not supposed to say.

You Must Accept Correction

Do not correct a scoffer, lest he hates you; rebuke a wise man, and he will love you. Give instruction

to a wise man, and he will still be wiser; teach a just man, and he will increase in learning.
—Proverbs 9:8–9, NKJV

A fool will never accept correction and become more foolish, but a wise man will take correction and become wiser and smarter. You must be teachable and humble to have the wisdom of God. You cannot act as if you know something if you do not know it. It is pride not to know something and say you know it. It is humility to accept that you don't know something and be ready to be teachable.

The Wise and Foolish Virgins

"Then the kingdom of heaven shall be likened to ten virgins who took their lamps and went out to meet the bridegroom. Now five of them were wise, and five were foolish. Those who were foolish took their lamps and took no oil with them, but the wise took oil in their vessels with their lamps. But while the bridegroom was delayed, they all slumbered and slept. "And at midnight a cry was heard: 'Behold, the bridegroom is coming; go out to meet him!' Then all those virgins arose and trimmed their lamps. And the foolish said to the wise, 'Give us some of your oil, for our lamps are going out.' But the wise answered, saying, 'No, lest there should not be enough for us and you; but go rather to those who sell, and buy for yourselves.' And while they went to buy, the bridegroom came, and those who were ready went in with him to the

wedding; and the door was shut. "Afterward the other virgins came also, saying, 'Lord, Lord, open to us!' But he answered and said, "Assuredly, I say to you, I do not know you.'

—Matthew 25:1–12, NKJV

Foolish people are always surprised. They are always caught unaware. Wise people are aware and not always surprised. The first five virgins were wise because they prepared themselves by having oil in their lamps. The other five virgins were foolish because they did not have oil in their lamp. They ended up losing their positions. Please prepare yourself for what God wants to do in your life so that you will not end up like these foolish virgins.

Hang Out with Wise People

He who walks with wise men will be wise, but the companion of fools will be destroyed.

—Proverbs 13:20, NKJV

If you walk with wise people, you will be wise, but if you walk with foolish people, you will become foolish. Your association is a powerful force that will shape your destiny. A good example is the disciples of Jesus Christ. The disciples of Jesus Christ were ignorant and illiterate before, but they talked with wisdom and boldness to the Pharisees when they were interrogated. They could do this because the same anointing and wisdom that was on Jesus Christ had rubbed off on them because they hung out with him (Acts 4:13).

Therefore, if you want the anointing and the wisdom of God to increase in your life, please hang out with real anointed men and women of God with God's wisdom. Another example is the relationship between Moses and Joshua, his assistant. Joshua served Moses with excellence. He hung out with him every time. The same anointing and wisdom that was on Moses had rubbed off on Joshua. Deuteronomy 34:9, NKJV confirms this: "Now Joshua the son of Nun was full of the spirit of wisdom, for Moses had laid his hands on him; so the children of Israel heeded him, and did as the LORD had commanded Moses."

Another good example is David and his followers. Some people joined David and asked him to be their leader, but the problem with them was that they were in distress, in debt, and were discontented about life (1 Samuel 22:2). After many years they had been with David, the same anointing and power that was on David's life had rubbed off on them. They became men of wisdom and great warriors. 2 Samuel 23:8-10, NKJV confirms this:

> *These are the names of the mighty men whom David had: Josheb-Basshebeth the Techmonite, chief among the captains. He was called Adino the Eznite because he had killed eight hundred men at one time. And after him was Eleazar the son of Dodo, the Ahohite, one of the three mighty men with David when they defied the Philistines who were gathered for battle, and the men of Israel had*

retreated. He arose and attacked the Philistines until his hand was weary, and his hand stuck to the sword. The LORD brought a great victory that day; and the people returned after him only to plunder.

Wisdom is Equal to Riches

*Length of days is in her right hand, in
her left hand riches and honor.*

—Proverbs 3:16, NKJV

The more wisdom you have, the richer you will be, and you will also live longer. Wisdom and riches go along together. God asked Solomon what he wanted God to do for him after offering one thousand offerings to God (2 Chronicles 1:6–7). He answered God in verse 7 that God should give him wisdom and knowledge to lead the people. God blessed him with wisdom and with prosperity (2 Chronicles 1:11–12). This is because wisdom will always come with riches and wealth. Solomon also achieved greatness. If you want to prosper, please seek the wisdom of God.

14

WORSHIP

Oh, sing to the LORD a new song! Sing to the LORD, all the earth. Sing to the LORD, bless his name; Proclaim the good news of His salvation from day to day. Declare His glory among the nations, His wonders among all peoples. For the LORD is great, and greatly to be praised; He is to be feared above all gods. For all the gods of the peoples are idols, But the LORD made the heavens. Honor and majesty are before Him; Strength and beauty are in His sanctuary.

—Psalms 96:1–6 (KJV)

Worship means attributing values and giving praises to God all the time. It is also an act of reference to God and submission to Him in all areas of our lives. Worship is giving God the permission to take control of our lives. It is a powerful tool for entering the presence of God. God is a King and must be worshipped, appreciated, and celebrated. God wants His children to worship Him in truth and in spirit. Worshipping God is our reason for living.

Worship is an act of love to God. If you are obedient to God, it is an act of worship to Him. If you help people that need help, it is an act of worship to God. If you forgive people that hurt you, it is an act of worship to Him. If you are taking care of your father and mother, it is an act of worship to God. If you pray for your leaders, it is an act of worship to Him. If you love your neighbors as yourself, it is an act of worship to God. Worshipping God covers different areas of our lives.

We can worship God in many ways. We can worship Him with our lifestyle. We can worship God in our hearts and by singing songs to Him, and also through our offerings. Christians must live a life of worship to be established and fulfilled in God.

God Is Worthy to Be Worshipped

MAKE a joyful noise unto the LORD, all ye lands. Serve the LORD with gladness: come before his presence with singing. Know ye that the LORD he is God: it is he that hath made us, and not we ourselves; we are his people, and the sheep of his pasture. Enter into his gates with thanksgiving, and into his courts with praise: be thankful unto him, and bless his name. For the LORD is good; his mercy is everlasting; and his truth endureth to all generations.

—Psalms 100:1–5 (KJV)

God is worthy to be worshipped and greatly to be praised. When you worship God, you will have access to His presence. God is the Creator of the universe. He is the Commander in Chief of heaven and the earth. He is the Absolute Ruler of the Universe. He is the Prince of Peace. He is the King of Salem. He is the Prince of Salem. Everything will bow down before God. Everything on earth, under the earth, in heaven will bow down and worship God. He is the Father of Glory. He is a God of greatness and a source of greatness. He is the source of dominion and God of dominion. He is more than powerful. He is more than precious. He is more than miraculous. He is more than special. He is the real deal. All adoration, all glory, all power, all dominion, all righteousness belong to God. He is the Ancient of Days. Worship God in the beauty of His Holiness.

Weakness, mediocrity, lies, illusion, delusion, confusion, contamination, jealousy, resentment, sickness, sin, death, unforgiveness, laziness, indifference, deception, and so on cannot be found in Him. Righteousness, holiness, wisdom, and power are the foundation of His kingdom. He is the Almighty God. He is the Father of Glory. We must continue to thank and worship God for His everlasting mercy upon our lives. We must worship God for putting the seed of greatness in us. We must worship God because of who He is and what He has done for us. We have a reason to bless God and appreciate Him.

Real Worship Will Touch God's Heart

But the hour cometh, and now is, when the true worshipers shall worship the Father in spirit and truth: for the Father seeketh such to worship him. God is a spirit: and those who worship him must worship him in spirit and truth.

—John 4: 23–24 (KJV)

Real worship will always touch God's heart. Real worship is when you do not feel like worshipping God because of your problems or your circumstances, but you worship Him anyway. Real worship is an act of faith to move the hands of God. God always shows up during the real worship. Two good examples are the apostles Paul and Silas. The magistrates put them in jail, and they started worshipping God. God visited them and delivered them (Acts 16: 20–33).

Real worship will always bring deliverance to God's people. Paul and Silas had the opportunity to escape when the doors of the prison were opened, and the chain they used to bound them were loosed, but they stayed there. When the keeper of the prison woke up and saw what happened, he wanted to kill himself because he thought they had escaped.

Paul screamed to him not to kill himself because they were still there. The man now asked a profound question when he saw the power of God in Acts 16:30, NKJV: "Sirs, what must I do to be saved?" They told him in Acts 16:31, NKJV, "Believe on the Lord Jesus Christ, and you will be saved, you and your household." Therefore, the man and his household gave their lives to Jesus Christ. This was possible because apostles Paul and Silas worshipped God. Real worship will always touch God's heart.

True worshipers will always worship God in the spirit. How can you worship God in the spirit? You can worship God in the spirit by taking your mind off the flesh and the world and focus on only Him. You cannot receive anything from God by worshiping Him in your flesh. If you want to experience God's supernatural power through your worship, please worship Him in truth and in spirit.

Worship Will Give You Long Life

In those days was Hezekiah sick unto death. And Isaiah the prophet, the son of Amoz came unto him, and said unto him, Thus saith the LORD, Set thine house in order: for thou shalt die, and not live. And said, Remember now, O LORD, I beseech thee, how I have walked before thee in truth and with a perfect heart, and have done that which is good in thy sight. And Hezekiah wept sore. For the grave cannot praise thee, death cannot celebrate thee: they that go down into the pit cannot hope for thy truth. The living, the living, he shall praise thee, as I do this day: the father to the children shall make known thy truth. The LORD was ready to save me: therefore we will sing my songs to the stringed instruments all the days of our lives in the house of the LORD.

— Isaiah 38:1-3, 18-20 (KJV)

Hezekiah got the bad news from prophet Isaiah that God said he should set his house in order because he would die. He wept and reminded God how he walked before Him with a perfect heart. He told God that the dead cannot praise Him or hope for His truth, but only the living can worship Him. He said that if God spares his life, he would worship God. When God heard that he would worship Him if He saves his life, God quickly told Isaiah to go back and tell Hezekiah that He heard his prayers and added fifteen years to his life. Worship was what gave Hezekiah a long life. If you want to live long and achieve greatness, I will encourage you to stop complaining and start worshipping God in truth and in spirit.

Three powerful nations declared war against Jehoshaphat and the children of God. They wanted to destroy them. Jehoshaphat proclaimed a fast among the people. They gathered together in God's presence and prayed for God's help because they did not have the strength to fight these great armies. Jehoshaphat specifically told God that, "we have no might against this great company that cometh against us; neither know we what to do: but our eyes are upon thee" (2 Chronicles 20:12, KJV). They totally depended on God because they could not help themselves. God gave them a Word through Jahaziel. This was what he said, "Hearken ye, all Judah, and ye inhabitants of Jerusalem, and thou king Jehoshaphat, Thus saith the LORD unto you, Be not afraid nor dismayed by reason of this great multitude: for the battle is not yours but God's" (2 Chronicles 20:15, KJV). On the day of the battle, Jehoshaphat appointed singers, and all of them worshipped God with everything in them. As they were praising God, God sent ambushment against their enemies. They destroyed one another. Not one of them escaped. All the enemies were dead by the time Jehoshaphat and the children of God got to where they were. It took three days to gather the spoils of the enemies (2 Chronicles 20:17-26). This happened because they worshipped God. Worship will give you rest, but it is a weapon of mass destruction that will destroy your enemies. Worship will make your battle easy, and also help you to achieve greatness.

Prayer of Salvation

An intimate relationship with God through His Son is the key to a fulfilled and victorious life. If you want to give meaning to your life, your time has come to accept Jesus Christ as your personal Lord and Savior. I am going to give you a deal of a lifetime, and the deal is that your time has come to accept Jesus Christ as your Lord and Savior. Please pray this prayer with me:

Heavenly Father, I accept the fact that I am a sinner. I confess my sins before you, and I choose to turn away from my sins. I ask you to cleanse me of all my sins of unrighteousness. I believe that Jesus Christ came into this world and died for my sins and resurrected on the third day. Today, I accept Jesus Christ into my life as my Lord and Savior. Jesus Christ, I will follow you for the rest of my life. I declare I am a born-again child of God in Jesus' name. Amen.

If you pray that simple prayer by faith, I believe you have been born again. I encourage you to attend a good church where the Word of God is explained, and only Jesus Christ is magnified.

Printed in the United States
By Bookmasters

Printed in the United States
By Bookmasters